IMAGES
of America

FORT JACKSON

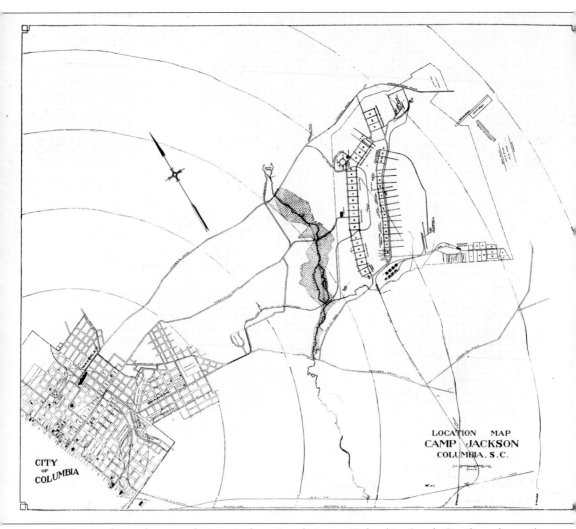

This map shows the area of Camp Jackson in relation to Columbia, South Carolina: four miles northeast of the city limits on Wild Cat Road between Garner's Ferry Road and Camden Road. More than 2,700 acres were obtained, including land that formerly belonged to Wade Hampton, Confederate general and later South Carolina governor and senator. (Author's collection.)

ON THE COVER: This 1948 photograph of a field training exercise (FTX) shows troops in action as they utilize the skills learned during the course of training. The exercise gives soon-to-be soldiers a taste of battle before leaving basic training, and it also allows drill instructors to evaluate the quality and effectiveness of their instruction. (Courtesy of Basic Combat Training Museum.)

IMAGES
of America

FORT JACKSON

David Galassie

ARCADIA
PUBLISHING

Published by Arcadia Publishing
Charleston, South Carolina

Printed in the United States of America

Library of Congress Control Number: 2019946132

For all general information, please contact Arcadia Publishing:
Telephone 843-853-2070
Fax 843-853-0044
E-mail sales@arcadiapublishing.com
For customer service and orders:
Toll-Free 1-888-313-2665

Visit us on the Internet at www.arcadiapublishing.com

*To Teresa, as always, a source of inspiration and
a constant supporter of my efforts.*

CONTENTS

ACKNOWLEDGMENTS

I would like to express my deepest gratitude to museum director Henry Howe and Darcie Fouste of the US Army Basic Combat Training Museum. Their support in providing access to photographs and pointing me in the right direction was priceless.

Special thanks to Dr. Steve Bower, US Army Soldier Support Institute historian and great supporter. His wisdom and knowledge of military history aided me tremendously, and his comprehensive edit helped in shaping this work.

I am indebted to the great editors at Arcadia Publishing, particularly Chad Rhoad, who helped refine my idea, and Stacia Bannerman, who nurtured this book to fruition. Their generous help throughout this process helped to realize this dream.

Thanks to Bob Johnstone and to Lt. Col. Carl Kleinholz for their steadfast support of my projects.

And special thanks to my wife, Teresa, who gave me the idea for this book, and for allowing me to indulge my passion for all things historical.

Unless otherwise noted, all photographs appear courtesy of the Basic Combat Training Museum.

INTRODUCTION

Before Fort Jackson, there was Camp Jackson. The onset of America's involvement in World War I, or the Great War as it was then known, necessitated the construction of several camps across the United States to recruit and train troops to fight for Uncle Sam "over there." Columbia, South Carolina, had had a love-hate relationship with federal troops since the close of the Civil War. As a part of Reconstruction, Columbia hosted a military force until 1877. Later, in the build-up to the Spanish-American War in 1898, five tent camps were built around Columbia. Apparently, this experience was a good one, for the Columbia city fathers took notice and sought out a more permanent military installation near the city.

In advance of World War I and with only 124,000 active-duty troops, the Army was in no position to make a big impact to the Allied effort in Europe. Congress instituted the Selective Service Act in 1917 and required adult men aged 21 to 30 to register for the draft to meet the manpower goals of the American Expeditionary Force commander, Gen. John J. Pershing. Existing facilities could not support the massive mobilization of manpower needed for the war effort. Consequently, the Army publicized its great need to build several military facilities across the United States, including nine National Guard camps and three National Army cantonments in the southeastern part of the country.

Columbia's chamber of commerce entered the fray, contacting Maj. Gen. Leonard Wood, the regional commander, to express its interest in hosting an installation. In turn, Major General Wood sent Maj. C.E. Kilbourne to inspect the area and make an assessment in January 1917. By May 19, Columbia had appointed a Cantonment Committee, raised $50,000 to buy 1,192 acres that could be donated to the government, secured options for leasing another 1,545 acres to the Army at $5 per acre per year, and celebrated its designation as the site of one of the new Army training camps. In all, the committee had arranged for the purchase of 2,737 acres four miles from the city limits on Wild Cat Road between Garner's Ferry Road and Camden Road. Special considerations that Columbia offered were included in the agreement with the Army. That included a guarantee from merchants that their prices would be the same for Army personnel as for Columbia citizens, a guarantee from the Columbia street railway company that a trolley line would extend from Columbia to the camp site with a fare less than 5¢, and invitations from local clubs to Army officers. From the onset, as seen in this agreement, Columbia was determined to make its relationship with the Army into something wholesome and above-board. That is still the environment today, as visitors to Fort Jackson can readily see that the post is not surrounded by the stereotypical trappings and purveyors of vice and licentious behavior that seem to take root around other military installations.

After the Great War ended, Camp Jackson entered a period of demobilization. Divisions were deactivated, and nearly 2,000 buildings, including quarters, warehouses, exchanges, and the like, were doomed to the wrecking ball. Land that had been leased to the federal government reverted to its former owners, and the original land that had been contributed by Columbia's citizenry was turned over to a Cantonment Lands Commission for educational, recreational, and industrial use. The Boy Scouts and Girls Scouts established camps on the land. Camp Jackson was formally closed pursuant to War Department General Order No. 33, dated July 27, 1921.

In 1925, when the War Department decided that the land would be once again useful, this time for South Carolina National Guard training, the dismantling of Camp Jackson's infrastructure was still ongoing. This was quickly halted—half of the camp's land was given over to the state of South Carolina in a revocable license, and certain buildings were constructed and improvements were financed by the National Guard Bureau through the adjutant general of South Carolina. But, except for the two-week increments for National Guard training, the camp remained virtually deserted for much of the year.

Throughout the 1930s, Camp Jackson remained a bucolic, sleepy installation save for the National Guard activity. Then came Nazi Germany and its aggression in Europe. Seeing the escalating tensions in Europe and the declaration of war by its ally Great Britain, the United States hastened its efforts to upgrade military facilities. Camp Jackson was included. The camp was reactivated in late 1939 and became the temporary home of the 6th Infantry Division, ordered to duty in October of that year. New barracks, mess halls, and kitchens were quickly constructed, supplanting the National Guard facilities inadequate to support the nationwide mobilization effort. The next year, a new hospital was constructed, while the post hosted the reactivation and mobilization of the 8th Infantry Division. In July 1940, Camp Jackson was designated a fort by General Order No. 7. Issued by George C. Marshall, Army chief of staff, the general order enabled the investment of millions of dollars in infrastructure development—housing, exchanges, libraries, chapels, ranges, and over 100 miles of road construction. Before the end of the war, Fort Jackson would host the mobilization and training of the 77th Infantry Division, the 30th Infantry Division, the 757th Tank Battalion, and the 102nd Cavalry. In 1942, Britain's prime minister, Winston Churchill, visited the post and after surveying the troops was said to have remarked, "They're just like money in the bank."

With the end of World War II, Fort Jackson was put on standby status in 1950 as the nation entered the largest demobilization effort in its history. However, the United Nations' "police action" in Korea made Fort Jackson a beehive of activity once again. In 1956, at the height of the Cold War, the post was designated a US Army training center, a status it maintains to the present day. Since that time, Fort Jackson has achieved status as the largest basic training center in the US Army and has become the home of many other missions, including the Army's Drill Sergeant Academy.

Other missions include the US Army Soldier Support Institute (USASSI), an umbrella organization that includes the US Army Adjutant General School, the US Army Financial Management School, the USASSI Non-Commissioned Officer Academy, and the Inter-Service Postal Activity. Also calling Fort Jackson home are the US Army Chaplain Center and School, National Center for Credibility Assessment, Leader Training Brigade, 81st Regional Support Command, Naval Reserve Center, Military Entrance Processing Station, Columbia Recruiting Battalion, and more.

The advent of Fort Jackson has had a significant economic impact on Columbia and the surrounding area. Fort Jackson generates more than $2.2 billion per year for the state and local economy. According to a 2017 University of South Carolina study, Fort Jackson has 7,600 military and civilian employees. Moreover, each year, more than 100,000 parents, friends, and family members from all over the United States descend upon Columbia to attend basic training graduation activities and a whole host of other activities associated with the larger Fort Jackson mission. Consumer spending on airfare, lodging, restaurants, souvenirs, local attractions, and the like totals into the millions.

As you can see, there is much to know about Fort Jackson. Let's take a tour.

One

IN THE BEGINNING

Fort Jackson was created in 1917 as Camp Jackson as the United States entered World War I. At the conclusion of the war, the camp was shut down. It was abandoned on April 25, 1922, but reactivated for World War II. The post was to have been deactivated by 1950, but the Korean War caused it to remain active, and it is still functioning today.

This postcard, like the one on the previous page, is a photograph taken by Walter L. Blanchard, noted for his photography in Columbia. Notice the sign above identifying the tent in the foreground as the headquarters for the commander of the Motor Truck Company and, of course, the trucks below. The back of this card includes a message from an artillery soldier to his sweetheart in West Virginia.

In formation, the tents of Battery E, 1st Field Artillery, stand tall against the Carolina pines of Camp Jackson. Batteries are roughly equivalent to a company in the infantry and are combined into larger organizations—either battalions or regiments—for administrative and operational purposes, and may be grouped into brigades. During military operations, the role of artillery is to provide support to other arms in combat or to attack targets.

Maj. Gen. Charles J. Bailey was the second post commander for Camp Jackson, serving from October 1917 through May 1918. The 81st Infantry Division "Wildcats" had been organized as a national division of the Army at Camp Jackson in August 1917, and in 1918, General Bailey assumed command of the division in France during World War I. The 81st originated the idea of the unit patch that every soldier wears today.

Major General Bailey began his career as a graduate of the 1880 class of the US Military Academy at West Point. Primarily a coastal artillery officer, he saw action in the Spanish-American War as a battery commander of field artillery. Prior to his service at Camp Jackson, from 1914 to 1917, he commanded the coastal defenses of Manila and Subic Bay in the Philippines.

This July 1918 panoramic view of the eastern section of Camp Jackson clearly shows the trolley line promised by the City of Columbia when the deal was finalized for the camp's land with the federal government. The photographer was John Allen Sargeant, who once had been an assistant to Walter L. Blanchard. During World War I, he served as camp photographer at Camp Jackson,

and after the war, he opened his own studio on Main Street in Columbia. The clarity of the trees, building, and vehicles in the photograph is in drastic contrast to the blurring of the trolley in motion, which, due to slower shutter speeds in the cameras of the era and longer exposure times, could not be captured in that instant. (Courtesy of Library of Congress.)

This view of troops encircling their instructor shows the spartan nature of early Camp Jackson. Dirt roads, wooden buildings, and sand everywhere were the watchwords for those conscripted into military service. No one ever said it would be easy, but these trainees in the hot, humid South, especially those unlucky to be stationed here from northern climes, had an especially hard go of it.

They say a soldier's weapon is his best friend, and its condition will be inspected over and over. He does not want his gun to jam or malfunction when he needs it most, so the soldier disassembles and maintains it until he can practically do it in his sleep. Many a trainee, instead of counting sheep, did just that.

From October 1917 until May 1918, the 318th Field Signal Battalion trained carrier pigeons while at Camp Jackson. From the dawn of time until the advent of reliable radio, pigeons were used for carrying messages for military units. During the two world wars, pigeons were used to transport messages back to their home coop behind the lines. When they landed, wires in the coop would sound a bell or buzzer, and a soldier would know a message had arrived. He would go to the coop, remove the message from the canister, and send it to its destination via telegraph, field phone, or personal messenger. Pigeons were so celebrated that a famous one named President Wilson who served in Europe is now on display outside the Army chief of staff's office in the Pentagon.

Until the Second World War, horses and mules were a vital part of the Army's transportation assets. This horse corral is a part of what was known as the remount station at Camp Jackson. These stations across the Army's camps varied widely in size, but the largest was at Camp Jackson, with a capacity of about 10,000 animals. Most others were in the 4,000–5,000 range.

This photograph shows the mule corral, and gives a sense of how extensive the animal population was at Camp Jackson. The Army owned only a few thousand horses and mules in 1917, when the United States entered World War I. There was thought to be an abundant supply in the civilian world that could be made available on short notice if needed.

Camp Jackson soldiers got their chance to dig and train in trenches. Trench warfare was widespread on the western front during World War I. Using occupied fighting lines consisting largely of military trenches, the troops were well-protected from the enemy's small arms fire and were substantially sheltered from artillery fire.

Trench warfare in World War I was mostly a hellish affair—the noise from artillery shells was deafening, and the trenches often filled with water, possibly leading to trench foot, a malady from the standing water soldiers lived in for long periods of time. The trenches were more involved than what is shown here; zig-zagged trench lines extended into a network of command posts, supply depots, and rest stations.

Airing the beds from the barracks might be seen as regular housekeeping for living in such close quarters, but in the midst of involvement in World War I, a worldwide influenza pandemic took hold in July 1918 and lasted for well over a year, claiming the lives of over 43,000 troops. The Army's medical department actually prescribed this tactic to bolster the health of troops.

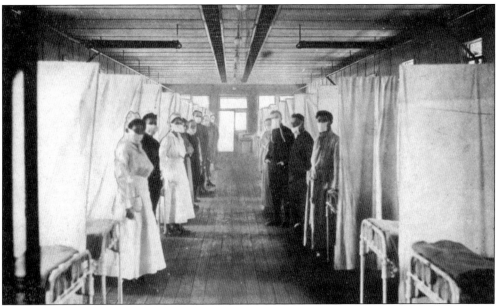

The influenza pandemic often required troops' hospitalization. Concerned with the importance of contact and droplet infections in the spreading of airborne diseases, the medical department took it upon itself to minimize the danger by requiring the use of cubicles for the patients and masks and gowns in hospitals. As shown here, the Camp Jackson hospital followed this protocol, hanging sheets to create the cubicles.

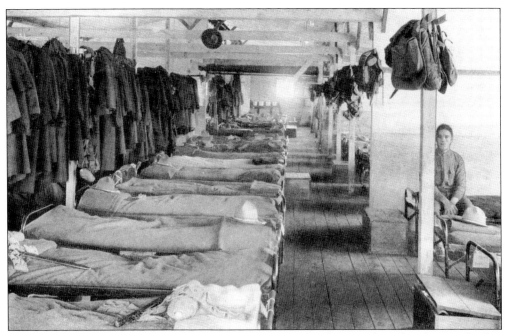

The close proximity of bunkmates, as shown in this barracks photograph, makes the case for that medical department policy of airing out mattresses. There was no privacy here and little room as well, as bunk beds were just coming into fashion. In later years, wall lockers and footlockers would become necessities for barracks life.

The smiles on these soldiers' faces might be more sincere than one would expect. With the draft came men from all socioeconomic backgrounds. Before their service, some might have even dined with finger bowls and had valets to wait upon them, while others were not used to regular meals. To them, this might have been the best grub they had ever eaten.

The 371st Infantry Regiment formed in August 1917 and was made up of African American draftees, mostly from South Carolina, and white officers. After training at Camp Jackson, the unit arrived on the western front in April 1918. The regiment was placed under the French Army's command because it desperately needed new troops and because of fear that racial tension might erupt between black and white American soldiers. The 371st was given French equipment, including French rifles. The unit was reorganized to fit the French Army structure and spent the spring of 1918 training in French tactics, communicating via interpreters. Distinguishing itself with meritorious service, the 371st was awarded the French Legion of Honor and the Croix de Guerre, and the Distinguished Service Cross was awarded to 10 officers and 12 enlisted men. One soldier, Cpl. Freddie Stowers, was eventually awarded the Medal of Honor.

Two

Troop Life

Soldiers line up for mess in front of the barracks. The mess hall and kitchen facilities were on the first floor of this building, while living quarters were on the second floor. All the soldiers carry their mess kits and are in the uniform of the era. One soldier is wearing the wide-brimmed campaign hat.

Troops were responsible for their own cleanup after chowing down at the mess hall. These soldiers wait their turn to wash and rinse their mess kits. At the far end of the line is a receptacle for uneaten food. Most of these troops are wearing their campaign hats. Notice the elaborate lacing on their leggings.

Pictured here are the regimental officers' quarters. While by today's standards these buildings seem unexceptional, they would have been viewed as the height of luxury by the enlisted men confined to their own close-quartered barracks. First built when the camp was established, by the end of 1917, there were 119 quarters capable of housing 1,700 officers.

Physical activity was not reserved just for the enlisted soldiers; officers got into the act as well. Use of the medicine ball was typical for the era, though it dates to ancient times. Gymnasiums were equipped with such balls, along with Indian clubs and rowing machines. Notice the mattresses being aired out from the windows of the barracks.

Pictured here is a regimental band that provided music during official events—military funerals, changes of command, and promotion ceremonies. The bands were often used to conduct public performances in support of recruitment activities such as street parades and concerts, and they provided popular music to entertain deployed military personnel. Bands of this era often featured 36 members, though there appear to be fewer in this photograph.

In the early 20th century, sheet music was a staple in every home, as was a piano in the parlor. So is it any wonder that music would be used to help boost soldiers' morale? This postcard shows a singing class for soldiers. "Song cards" were also given to troops that contained lyrics and, on their reverse, invited them to music performances in Columbia.

When the training day was over, there was also time for command-sanctioned sports. Often this would entail a boxing match, a baseball game, or some other exhibition that would rouse the troops' interest and allow them some relief from the grueling training activities of the day.

The Liberty Theatre was part of a morale and welfare concept inspired by the US government to establish national theaters at the 16 new Army cantonments. Each theater was built to identical specifications and held 3,000 patrons. A 16-week circuit was established with legitimate performers who would travel among the training camps. Four comedies, four vaudeville shows, and eight local talent shows were the lineup.

In later years, as movies became more popular, the post maintained seven movie theaters, one of which is pictured here. These buildings were also used for touring USO camp shows. The latest movies were shown for a small admission fee. Hollywood filmed countless training movies for the Army and the war-production industry. Movies aided in familiarizing soldiers with foreign terrain, identifying aircraft, and simulating combat.

During World War I, at the invitation of the federal government, the Young Women's Christian Association established what were known as "hostess houses" at American military camps and employed women as hostesses. These houses helped facilitate interactions between soldiers and their female friends and relatives, as it had become known that there were numerous obstacles in making these connections. The YWCA established 50 houses at 37 different military installations.

The connection between the YMCA and the American military goes back to the Civil War, so it was no surprise with the advent of World War I that the YMCA offered its services. The YMCA provided activities and services that varied by location but usually included recreation (sports, films, concerts, and singing), library services, religious services, and the sale of refreshments, cigarettes, and other personal items.

The Knights of Columbus were not to be outdone by the YMCA's initiative in taking care of the troops. While the YMCA prided itself as a Protestant organization that tried to leave religion out of the recreation equation, the Knights of Columbus took it upon themselves to be the defenders of Catholic soldiers everywhere, and inadvertently created a fierce rivalry for the soldiers' attention.

The post library also played a major role in recreation for the soldier. On Valentine's Day 1918, both the post library and the YWCA Hostess House opened for business. The two were almost adjacent to each other—the Knights of Columbus house sat in between. Also nearby was the Liberty Theatre.

No. 1668   Typical Chapel and Church Service—
Fort Jackson, S. C.   (Photo by U. S. Army Signal Corps)

It is said that there are no atheists in foxholes. But whether or not that is accurate, the post abounds with chapels, and religious faiths of many denominations are represented. Religion is one means for soldiers to make sense of the world with everything going on around them. (Author's collection.)

This is a humorous postcard, likely sold in the post exchange, for soldiers to provide some lightheartedness to the folks back home. The realization of coping with the newfound realities of life in the Army was a common theme of such cards. No doubt countless variations of a cartoon like this made their way to homes across the land. (Author's collection.)

This postcard is a novel item from the World War II era. It originally was a matchbook but then could be used as a postcard when the matches were all depleted. The back cover depicts the various branch insignia that were represented as training or having another presence at Fort Jackson. (Author's collection.)

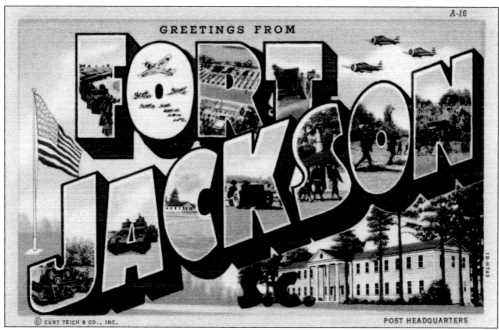

This large-letter postcard is typical for the 1930s and 1940s. Each letter provides space for different scenes of the overall location. This way, the buyer got the most bang for his buck, so to speak, as it provided multiple views on one card. The festive stars and stripes in the background round out a quite patriotic card fit for any Fort Jackson soldier to send home. (Author's collection.)

This postcard shows a multitude of views and served as a welcome, calming introduction to his family when "Private Snuffy" sent it home after arriving at basic training. Playing up the leisure activities afforded soldiers in the midst of their training served to smooth over anxious feelings his parents might have experienced. (Author's collection.)

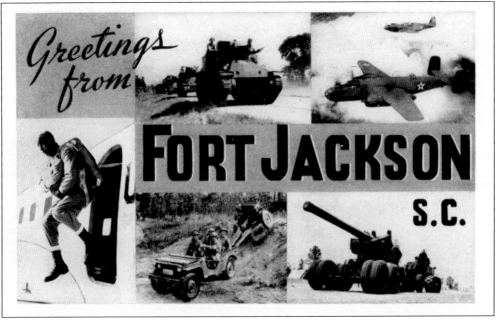

This postcard has more of a macho feel, containing activities unlikely to be found at Fort Jackson, including jumping out of airplanes and the Army Air Corps' fleet of bombers filling the skies. The simple explanation is that this was a collection of military photographs a publisher purchased and then printed the name of a military post on the front. It is a safe bet that many installations sold this card. (Author's collection.)

Three

AROUND TOWN

South Carolina's state capital was not initially called Columbia. Various name options were considered, including Washington, but Columbia won out in a state senate vote by a margin of 11 to 6. Columbia was primarily selected as the capital due to its location near the geographical center of the state. It became the capital in 1786. (Author's collection.)

The South Carolina State House, pictured here, is the second capital building Columbia has seen. The first was built between 1786 and 1790. An improved facility was initiated in earnest in 1855 after an abortive attempt four years earlier, but with the Civil War, construction understandably slowed. When troops under General Sherman occupied Columbia in 1865, the old statehouse was burned, and the interior of the new facility was gutted. To this day, one can view where artillery shells hit the new statehouse, as the locations are marked by bronze stars. The grounds of the statehouse are home to many monuments devoted to heroes of the Revolutionary and Civil Wars, including Gen. Wade Hampton. Until 2000, the Confederate battle flag flew above the statehouse, but it was taken down and moved to a special monument on the grounds. In 2015, in what is still considered a controversial move by some South Carolinians, the flag was removed from the grounds. (Both, author's collection.)

Columbia College was established in 1854 by the Methodist Church as a liberal arts, all-women's college. The college survived the march of General Sherman's troops through Columbia in 1865 by the audacious defiance of its music professor, W.H. Orchard. Renowned artist Georgia O'Keeffe taught art here from 1914 to 1915 before moving to New York. The college's daytime curriculum is still all-female, but its evening program has evolved to include coed graduate programs. (Author's collection.)

Five Points gets its name from the intersection of Harden Street, Devine Street, and Santee Avenue. As Columbia's first neighborhood shopping district, it saw many firsts, including Columbia's first supermarket, first Chinese restaurant, and first bar to serve a cocktail. It has evolved to a college entertainment district for area students but still maintains a family atmosphere as home of the annual St. Patrick's Day parade and celebration. (Author's collection.)

Columbia's William Jennings Bryan Dorn Veterans Administration Medical Center is located at 6439 Garners Ferry Road in the southeastern portion of the Columbia metropolitan area. The medical campus was originally completed in 1932, with additions in 1937, 1945, and 1946. A teaching hospital, the VA medical center is also home of the University of South Carolina's School of Medicine. (Author's collection.)

This Richland County Courthouse was completed in 1937 at a cost of $305,000. Constructed of Indiana limestone and Richland County brick, the interior was finished in oak. There was a total of 54 office rooms in addition to the county and circuit courtrooms. By the early 1970s, this facility had outlived its usefulness as the county's judicial center, and in 1980, a new judicial center at Main and Blanding Streets opened. (Author's collection.)

Located at 1705 Hampton Street, this was the boyhood home of Pres. Woodrow Wilson from about 1871 to 1875, when the family moved to Wilmington, North Carolina. Wilson's father, the Reverend Joseph Ruggles Wilson, was a professor at the Columbia Theological Seminary and minister of the First Presbyterian Church during these years. (Author's collection.)

Millwood was built by the first Wade Hampton, a brigadier general in the War of 1812. When he died in 1835, he was one America's wealthiest men, with plantations in several states. Allegedly burned by Union troops during the Civil War, all that remained of the original house were 12 columns and some outbuildings. Over time, this has been reduced to three round columns and two square columns. (Author's collection.)

First Baptist Church and Sunday School Building, Columbia, S. C.

The First Baptist Church, located at 1306 Hampton Street, was built in 1859 and was the home of the secession convention of 1860 that saw South Carolina leave the Union. It was the largest gathering place of its time. The church was spared burning by Sherman's army because the sexton misdirected troops to the Washington Street Methodist Church, which was burned instead. (Author's collection.)

This bridge was built in 1927 as the third span over the Congaree River and joins Gervais Street in Columbia with the city limits of West Columbia. This is part of the Jefferson Davis Highway, which was a series of designations for various highways stretching from coast to coast through the southern United States. The original bridge was destroyed by Confederate cavalry, who set it aflame on February 16, 1865. (Author's collection.)

Lake Murray Dam is only one name for the dam that created Lake Murray between 1927 and 1930. Formally known as the Dreher Shoals Dam, its construction necessitated the displacement of over 5,000 residents in nine communities that eventually ended up underwater after they were abandoned. Covering 50,000 acres, the lake encompasses 500 miles of shoreline. The Lake Murray Dam and its namesake lake hold many significant firsts: when completed in 1930, this was the world's largest earthen dam, and Lake Murray was deemed the world's largest man-made lake. During World War II, a B-25 bomber was lost in the waters of Lake Murray on a training flight and was never recovered in total. In 2005, a portion of the wreckage was retrieved, and it is now on display at the Southern Museum of Flight in Birmingham, Alabama. (Both, author's collection.)

The South Carolina Governor's Mansion was built in 1855 as part of the Arsenal Military Academy, one of two military academies in the state. The Arsenal Academy ceased operations with the Civil War, and after the war, this residence, the only Arsenal Academy building to survive the Union Army's occupation of Columbia, became the official governor's residence. Most governors since 1868 have resided here, save for two who lived in their existing Columbia residences. (Author's collection.)

The Township Auditorium, at 1703 Taylor Street, was built in 1930 and for years has been an important stop for entertainers visiting Columbia. Among the big-name entertainers to put on shows here were Elvis Presley, Ray Charles, B.B. King, Bill Haley and His Comets, Johnny Cash, Otis Redding, and James Brown. The Township was renovated in 2009 and remains an important cog in Columbia's entertainment scene. (Author's collection.)

The Wade Hampton III monument was dedicated on November 20, 1906, on the grounds northeast of the South Carolina State House. Surrounding the statue's base are 12 bronze plaques commemorating the battles in which Hampton fought. When the statehouse grounds were redone in the late 1960s, the statue was relocated to the front of the Wade Hampton Office Building, shown below in October 1969. Wade Hampton III was a member of the South Carolina House of Representatives from 1852 to 1856 and a state senator from 1858 to 1861. He served in the Confederate army during the Civil War, raising and commanding Hampton's Legion. He was wounded three times and was promoted to brigadier general in 1862, major general in 1863, and lieutenant general in 1865. Hampton served as governor of South Carolina from 1876 to 1879 and was elected in 1878 as a Democrat to the US Senate. He served from March 4, 1879, until March 3, 1891. He was unsuccessful in getting reelected to a third term but was US railroad commissioner from 1893 to 1897. Wade Hampton III died in Columbia on April 11, 1902. (Both, author's collection.)

Located at 910 Sumter Street, this old library on the university's quadrangle is the first separate college library in the United States, designed in 1840 by Robert Mills. The library became a special collections library with the construction in 1940 of the university's new library building, which is now McKissick Museum and the University of South Carolina Visitors Center. (Author's collection.)

The World War Memorial sits on the campus of the University of South Carolina. It was constructed with the aid of federal Public Works Administration funds, and was completed in 1936. Not just a memorial to the war dead from the Great War, the building was designed to be office space and currently houses the university's publications division. (Author's collection.)

Columbia was laid out in a plan that provided wide streets intersecting at right angles. Like most towns, Main Street is the commercial hub of the city, a vital artery evoking commerce, savings, and the burgeoning economy. Originally known as Richardson Street, Main Street's name was changed after the Civil War. In the city's original plan, north-south streets were named after Revolutionary War generals, in this case Richard Richardson. As with many Main Streets in many towns in America, Columbia's experienced a major economic decline with the advent of suburban shopping malls and urban flight. But Columbia's Main Street has undergone a renaissance in the last few years and shows no sign of stopping anytime soon. (Both, author's collection.)

Owens Field, Columbia, S. C., Municipal Airport

Owens Field was the main airport serving Columbia before World War II. It was originally known as Columbia Municipal Airport and was dedicated on April 24, 1930. During World War II, the airport was used by the Army Air Corps' Third Air Force as a training field while also remaining a viable commercial airport. The airport still serves the general aviation community in Columbia. (Author's collection.)

C-140   One of the Lakes in Arcadia, a beautiful residential suburb, Columbia, S. C.

Families fleeing the fast life of Columbia moved northeast to what became the town of Arcadia Lakes in the early 1900s. Heralding the fact that it has seven lakes in one town, its status was certified by the state in 1959. Belying its status as a town, Arcadia Lakes shares a zip code with part of northeastern Columbia, and all locations in the town have Columbia mailing addresses. (Author's collection.)

Trinity Church, now known as Trinity Episcopal Cathedral, resides at 1100 Sumter Street, just east of the statehouse. The parish had a wooden church from its inception in 1812, making it the oldest church in Columbia. The cornerstone for the church pictured here was laid in August 1845. During Sherman's march through Columbia, the church survived, though the rectory burned. (Author's collection.)

First Presbyterian Church. Columbia. S. C.

The classically Gothic-designed First Presbyterian Church was built in 1854 and sits at 1324 Marion Street. Spared the carnage of Sherman's march, the original 180-foot spire was damaged in 1875 by a hurricane and rebuilt in 1885. It was damaged again in a 1910 fire and was rebuilt to be eight feet taller. The parents of Pres. Woodrow Wilson are buried in its cemetery. (Author's collection.)

St. Peter's Roman Catholic Church is also known as the Basilica of St. Peter, having been granted minor basilica status by the pope in 2018. Essentially this means that the church has been granted special status and ecclesiastical privileges. The parish has its origins in 1821, when the Charleston diocese sent priests to Columbia to minister to the Irish workers on a Columbia canal. This church building dates from 1907. (Author's collection.)

Until 1971, the South Carolina Supreme Court met in the statehouse. That year, the old US post office, pictured here, was reopened as the headquarters for the court. The state had purchased the building in 1966, when the new post office was built on Assembly Street. Construction for this building began in 1917, but materials were diverted for construction of Camp Jackson. The post office opened in 1921. (Author's collection.)

Columbia Hospital opened for business in 1892 as one of the first hospitals in Columbia. Today, it is one of the premier medical facilities in central South Carolina. Formerly known as Richland Memorial Hospital, it expanded its reach by combining with Greenville Health Systems of Greenville, South Carolina, in 1998. It adopted the name Prisma Health in 2017. (Author's collection.)

In its heyday, the Wade Hampton Hotel was billed as the "Hotel of Tomorrow." The Hampton was part of a nationwide association of innkeepers known as the Affiliated National Hotels, a hallmark of quality to look for when traveling. By the 1980s, the facility had found temporary new life as lodging for college students. It was imploded in July 1985 after 40 years of service. (Author's collection.)

The Hotel Columbia did not fare any better. One of a series of Barringer Hotels, managed by Laurence S. Barringer, this was part of a stable that included inns in Charlotte, North Carolina; Myrtle Beach and Greenville, South Carolina; and one in Augusta, Georgia. This site was imploded in 1971 to make way for a skyscraper. (Author's collection.)

The Jefferson Hotel, designed and built by Columbia entrepreneur and contractor John Jefferson Cain, stood at the corner of Main and Laurel Streets from 1913 until 1968. The hotel was built in 1912–1913 at a cost of $250,000. For 55 years, the Jefferson was Columbia's premier hotel, hosting conventions as well as more informal meetings among legislators. It was demolished in 1968. (Author's collection.)

Flipper Library of Allen University, Columbia, S. C.

Allen University originated in Cokesbury, South Carolina, as the Payne Institute in 1870, a school designed to educate free blacks, former slaves, and their children. Its founders were ministers of the African Methodist Episcopal Church (AME). Renamed to honor Bishop Richard Allen, the founder of the AME Church, the school moved to Columbia in 1880. While its original mission was to educate and train Methodist ministers and teachers, today, the school follows a more conventional curriculum. It resides directly across Taylor Street from the other significant black college in Columbia, Benedict College. (Both, author's collection.)

C-80 ALLEN UNIVERSITY, COLUMBIA, S. C.

Antisdel Chapel, Benedict College, Columbia, S. C. — K-67-D-5

Benedict College began in 1870 with the purchase of an 80-acre former plantation. Bathsheba Benedict, while serving with the Baptist Home Mission Society, came up with the money to fulfill her dream of educating former slaves. At first, the school's mission was to educate its students to work as ministers and teachers. Over time, the mission changed, and today, a full four-year curriculum is offered in many liberal arts areas. The name was changed from Benedict Institute to Benedict College in 1894. Despite the school's black focus, it was not until 1930 that the college had an African American president. (Both, author's collection.)

Four

THE 1940S

In August 1940, Camp Jackson became Fort Jackson via General Order No. 7, signed by George C. Marshall, Army chief of staff. Millions of dollars were appropriated to construct housing and headquarters buildings, including this gleaming white new post headquarters that opened for business on January 9, 1941. This view is no more, for the building was razed in 2015.

On September 16, 1940, the United States instituted the Selective Training and Service Act of 1940, which required all men between the ages of 21 and 45 to register for the draft. This was the first peacetime draft in US history. Those who were selected from the draft lottery were required to serve at least one year in the armed forces. Once the United States entered World War II, draft terms extended through the duration of the fighting. By the end of the war in 1945, fifty million men between the ages of 18 and 45 had registered for the draft, and 10 million had been inducted into the military.

One of the first things a new recruit does, even before the mandatory haircut and the issuing of uniforms and field gear, is taking the oath of enlistment, as follows per Title 10, US Code, Section 502: "I, (state name), do solemnly swear (or affirm) that I will support and defend the Constitution of the United States against all enemies, foreign and domestic; that I will bear true faith and allegiance to the same; and that I will obey the orders of the president of the United States and the orders of the officers appointed over me, according to regulations and the Uniform Code of Military Justice, so help me God." Army Regulation 601-210, Active and Reserve Components Enlistment Program, provides that the oath be administered in a dignified manner with the US flag prominently displayed near the officer giving the oath. The words "So help me God" may be omitted for recruits who desire to affirm rather than to swear to the oath.

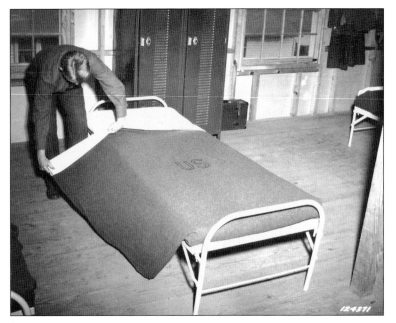

Regardless of the home situation from which the draftee came, he soon learned that there was the Army way and no other. And of course, this applied to the very bed or cot in which the new soldier slept. His drill sergeant demanded that crisp hospital corners and tightly pulled covers defined a well-made bed, as every soldier soon learned.

The housekeeping does not end with simply keeping one's personal space in sharp order. Too soon, the new soldier learns the phrase "GI party." Sadly, this does not mean beer and snacks and dance music but rather the use of electric polishers, mops, brooms, and floor wax by the barracks inhabitants, usually before an inspection.

Comic strips like *Beetle Bailey* and *Sad Sack* are rife with images of soldiers pushing mops or peeling potatoes as a sort of informal punishment for being incompetent. Even the television show *Gomer Pyle, USMC,* showed the Marine getting in trouble with his platoon sergeant and being taught a lesson by being handed over to the mess sergeant for extra duties. This sort of discipline was known as "KP," or "Kitchen Police." Formally known as "mess duty," the extra labor in reality often supplements personnel shortages in the dining facility more than serving as a means of getting a particular soldier's attention.

Marksmanship instructors measure the distances between the shots, which determines the proficiency of the shooter. There are four categories of marksmanship: unqualified, marksman, sharpshooter, and expert. Accordingly, qualification badges are awarded depending upon the attainment of these levels. These badges are not permanent; they vary based on performance. A soldier can qualify at the expert level one year and the next year have a bad qualification and finish as a marksman. The badges will change accordingly. Traditionally, in the US Army, only noncommissioned officers and enlisted personnel wear their badges on their service uniforms, despite them being awarded to officers as well.

There are three positions from which to fire a weapon: standing, kneeling, and prone. Pictured above is the supported prone position, the most basic. It also has the greatest potential for accurate shooting, since the front of the rifle rests nicely on a solid yet soft object—a forearm, a hat, or even a sandbag. This helps steady the rifle and absorbs recoil. Notice the group setting for this type of instruction. Most basic combat skills instruction comes in group format with the potential for one-on-one corrections later. This applies to everything from first aid to land navigation.

They say there are three things not to fool with: a soldier's mail, his pay, and his chow. Pictured here is mail call, something to look forward to and, occasionally, to fear, for many a soldier has witnessed his bunkmate receiving a Dear John letter. Of course, receiving much-anticipated news from mom and dad or a best girl certainly outweighs the alternative.

Before the age of "check to bank," ATM cards, and the like, soldiers used to engage in what were known as "payday activities." This would entail uniform inspections and some training perhaps, after which soldiers would walk to a designated day room and receive their pay in cash. Soldiers would then be allowed to go into town and pay their bills in person.

Field exercises and combat do not always allow for a mobile mess facility. In those cases, enter the field ration. In World War II, the predominant rations were known as C rations, or "C rats" to most. In the initial C ration, there were only three variations of the main course, labeled as an M-unit: meat and beans, meat and potato hash, or meat and vegetable stew. Also issued was one bread-and-dessert can, or B-unit. Each daily ration (enough food for one soldier for one day) consisted of six 12-ounce cans (three M-units and three B-units), while an individual meal consisted of one M-unit and one B-unit. Initially, C-Ration cans were marked with paper labels, which soon fell off, making a guessing game out of evening meals. After many complaints, manufacturers directly labeled the cans.

Pres. Franklin Roosevelt visited Fort Jackson on March 31, 1941, on his way from Florida to Washington, DC. The 35,000 troops training at the fort turned out to greet the commander in chief as he was given a private tour of the sprawling base. This visit was some nine months before the events of Pearl Harbor that propelled the United States into the thick of war. Yet political tensions filled the air, and preparations were taking place "just in case." With 1941 filled with military exercises and increased troop buildups, Fort Jackson was well-prepared to assume the greatly increased training loads the war required.

Prime Minister Winston Churchill visited Fort Jackson on June 24, 1942. Stepping off a train, he was accompanied by many major players in the war, including Secretary of War Henry L. Stimson, chief of staff Gen. George C. Marshall, and Lt. Gen. Lesley J. McNair, chief of Army ground forces. The assembled dignitaries witnessed a review of one regimental combat team from each of the three divisions of I Corps. Churchill tromped all over Fort Jackson, getting a taste of every facet of combat training the fort offered, unmistakable by the familiar cigar clenched between his teeth.

Official Army policy requires soldiers to shave unless medical necessity or religious conviction precludes it. Folliculitis is usually cited as the primary medical excuse to not shave. In recent years, Sikh soldiers have been allowed to maintain their beards. Out in the field, it can be challenging to maintain the clean-shaven look.

Personal hygiene is paramount for troops, especially in the field, and though it appears to be a humorous photo opportunity, this is serious. Depending upon the environment the soldier fights in, his very well-being can be challenged and compromised by ticks, chiggers, lice, and other parasites and airborne insects indigenous to the region. No one wants to be a casualty from non-combat-related health issues.

Gas mask training was a reality for troops in World War II. Memories of the crippling effects of mustard gas in World War I were still fresh in the military psyche, and no one was sure what the enemy was capable of. This photograph was taken early on in pre-war training at the fort. Notice the old-style doughboy helmets in use.

A rite of passage for every trainee was walking through the gas chamber. The experience was two-fold: it gave the soldier a chance to experience the protection his gas mask provided, but within moments of entering the chamber, the soldier was required to take the mask off and recite a general order to give him just enough exposure to truly appreciate his gas mask. It was cruel but effective.

Women performed duty in the armed forces during World War II to save on military manpower. As such, corps of women military members were created to complement each service. The Army's counterpart was the Women's Army Corps (WAC). Originally created as an auxiliary corps, the WACs were put into active service on July 1, 1943. While one would think the jobs available to women would be largely stereotyped activities such as typing, secretarial work, cooking, and baking, job opportunities increased as the war progressed through the addition of blue collar trades such as mechanics and weapons repair specialists.

Bayonet training is a combat skill that comes and goes out of fashion. After all, the last American bayonet charge occurred in the Korean War in 1951. But, as seen here during World War II, the training was still a requirement for each new recruit to impart the values of aggressiveness and courage for close combat with the enemy, though sometimes seen as a last resort.

The Army first introduced a formal fitness test in 1942. To get recruits in fighting shape, the Army implemented a physical development program as part of its combat basic training course. What became known as the Army Ground Forces Test was designed to assess whether the program was having its desired effect. The test included squat jumps, sit-ups, pull-ups, push-ups, and a 300-yard run.

Soldiers show their form in throwing hand grenades. The grenades used during World War II originated in the latter years of World War I, and this grenade became the de facto standard for American service members through the 1960s. Designed with markings that gave it the nickname of "pineapple," the grenade had a ring at the top protecting the pin and a five-second fuse, which gave the soldier enough time to hurl the grenade in the direction of the enemy. Internally, the grenade held two ounces of TNT and upon detonation would shower fragments of the iron casing in all directions within the blast radius.

Trench warfare was a holdover from World War I, where the entire western front in Europe was a series of trenches, as seen in chapter one. Despite its gradual decline as a defensive tactic due to the preponderance of tanks and armored vehicles, it was still taught at the beginning of World War II.

This charge by troops is likely dated from the early 1940s, judging by the uniforms in use. Specifically, use of the large campaign hats decreased as the war progressed, largely due to the costs and materials required for their manufacture. The hats never completely fell out of favor, as today's drill sergeants still employ them and are largely identified with them.

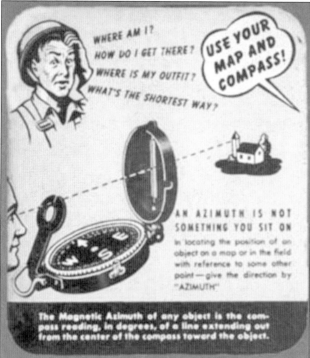

Needless to say, finding one's way on the battlefield using a map and a compass is a fundamental skill for anyone in the military. It is more than just a means of orienting oneself to the battlefield. Skill in land navigation is vital for calling in air and artillery support and is critical in extricating one's unit in particularly precarious situations.

This training aid works as a small refresher in the use of the lensatic compass. Essentially, without a protractor, one can place the compass on the map to approximate the needed bearing. Training aids like this were invaluable in serving as refreshers for weapons maintenance, radio procedures, and the like.

Looking like a scene from the Pacific theater, this field demonstration was held on July 2, 1942, by Company D, 105th Medical Battalion, as the men floated and towed a jeep wrapped in waterproof canvas across a Fort Jackson lake. Though more associated with the Marines, Army amphibious operations were one of the many skills taught during the World War II years.

Despite World War II's seemingly endless parade of technological advancements in communications, beginning Signal Corps soldiers are seen here working with headphones and telegraph keys, learning the fundamentals of Morse code. The war saw the rise of such innovations as static- and interference-free FM radio, channel-hopping, teletypewriters, walkie-talkies, and more.

In the photograph above, African American soldiers align themselves in formation using the commands "dress right, dress" and "ready, front." On the former command, the first squad leader stands fast and serves as the base. Other squad leaders obtain correct distance by estimation. The members of the first squad execute in the same manner as in squad drill to obtain exact intervals. All other squads execute as the first squad, except that each squad member raises the left arm only for uniformity, actually covering on the man to the front. Patriotic African Americans wanting to do their part were involved with the war from the beginning, though prevailing attitudes in this era before Civil Rights legislation led to continued segregation of their units despite President Roosevelt signing a bill making discrimination in war industries and federal agencies illegal.

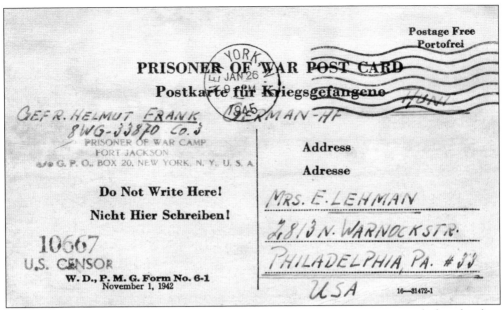

This press photograph from May 1944 features Cpl. Agatha Klump, who discusses a case with an unidentified coworker in the Discharge Section of the Military Personnel Office at Fort Jackson. Corporal Klump processed the paperwork of enlisted men about to be discharged, checking their dates of enlistment, discontinuing allotments, and the like. Photographs like this helped publicize the great work the WACs were doing on behalf of their country. (Author's collection.)

This photograph shows some of the 14,000 men of the 8th Infantry Division who massed on the parade grounds at Fort Jackson for Army Day festivities on April 7, 1941. Many relatives and friends visited from surrounding states to witness this and other special events during the open house that day.

Current hobbyists of flying drones might be surprised to learn that the use of unmanned aircraft dates to 1939. Pictured here is an anti-aircraft crew on November 1, 1943, sending up a radio-controlled airplane via catapult for target practice. If the aircraft survived, it was recovered using a parachute to bring it back to earth.

Two Japanese American soldiers man a machine gun. Pvt. Takeshi Omuro fires the weapon while PFC Kentoku Wakasone feeds the cartridge belt. This press photograph from 1943 described the two as seeking revenge for the Pearl Harbor attack on their Hawaiian Islands birthplace, while stressing their unwavering loyalty and patriotism to their country. They served honorably in spite of America's policy of forced relocation of Japanese American citizens to internment camps.

This 155-millimeter howitzer originated with the French during World War I. Using 100-pound shells, it had a maximum distance of seven miles. The United States bought the rights to the gun and modified it with rubber tires and a slightly different firing mechanism. Until its replacement in late 1942, this workhorse remained the standard American heavy howitzer. It was superseded by the 155-millimeter M1 howitzer.

The pass in review is a long-standing military tradition that began as a way for a commander to inspect his troops. It dates to the late 1700s, when Gen. George Washington brought Baron von Steuben to America to instill discipline and decorum in his troops. As the color guard passes the commander, other flags dip, while the US flag always remains erect.

This picture shows the ceremony known as retreat, which takes place at the close of each day. The evening gun is fired, the national anthem is played, and Old Glory is lowered from the flag staff and carefully folded. The flag security detail lowers the flag slowly and with dignity. If the flag is being flown at half-staff, it is raised briskly to the top then lowered slowly.

Five

THE COLD WAR

Fort Jackson Boulevard enters Fort Jackson at Gate One, for many years the main gate to the post. With the building of the interstate, main gate access eventually shifted about one mile to Gate Two, which connects to Forest Drive. Traffic backups become quite severe on Wednesdays and Thursdays due to basic training graduations, which led to increased visitor access for those events at Gate Four.

Just beyond the gate on the previous page is a traffic circle that, until recently, held a statue of Andrew Jackson, the seventh president of the United States and the namesake of the post. On November 11, 1970, the citizens of Columbia donated the $82,500, twelve-foot statue by sculptor Felix DeWeldon to Fort Jackson in recognition of the city's gratitude to the Army post. Also included were four side panels that illustrated scenes symbolizing wars fought in by soldiers trained at Fort Jackson: World War I, World War II, the Korean War, and the Vietnam War. In 2013, the statue was moved to Hilton Field in a remodel of the basic training graduation venue. The press photograph at left shows one of the post's drill sergeants saluting the flag during the dedication ceremony.

With the conclusion of World War II, Congress mandated that many of the military's posts be demobilized. Fort Jackson became a replacement training center, and most of the Army divisions associated with the post were deactivated. The famous 5th Division was reactivated in 1947 as a training division, and the 8th followed in 1950 when the Korean War broke out.

The 8th Division was reactivated on August 17, 1950, and resided on Fort Jackson until May 1954, when it was transferred to Camp Carson, Colorado. Its replacement was the famed 101st Airborne Division "Screaming Eagles," which stayed until March 1956, at which time it was sent to Fort Campbell, Kentucky. Pictured here is the 8th Division's pipe band, which consisted of bagpipers.

Post–World War II soldiers perform an impromptu last-minute inspection of their M1 rifles in front of their barracks. Until the late 1950s, this was the standard rifle for the Army. Seeing combat in World War II and in Korea, the M1 had a notable heritage. So it was no surprise when the next iteration of weaponry, the M14, evolved directly from the M1. In the photograph below of an inspection in progress, the soldiers wear the rarely seen khaki tropical summer uniform that included knee-high stockings and knee-length shorts. From about 1956 until 1959, this uniform was optional for summer wear by soldiers.

Pvt. Victoria Pucci of Glen Lyon, Pennsylvania, sends messages to the Third Army Headquarters as she operates her teletype machine in the message center on January 22, 1951. Teleprinters could send and receive messages without the need for operators trained in the use of Morse code. A system of two teleprinters, with one operator trained to use a typewriter, replaced two trained Morse code operators.

One of the Signal Corps' essential functions was to provide radio and phone communications during war, and that required stringing wires from telephone poles. A 1952 issue of *Combat Forces Journal* stated that pole climbers spent up to 21 hours mastering the art of pole climbing, starting at 10-foot poles and fearlessly working their way up to 35-foot poles.

Capt. Frederick M. Schweiger, from Northbrook, Illinois, performing advanced individual training (AIT) with the 340th Regiment, 85th Division, US Army Reserve, directs fire of a 106-millimeter M40 recoilless rifle crew at Fort Jackson during two weeks of summer training in July 1961. Notice the LBE, or load bearing equipment, of the soldiers standing by the vehicle. Each wears his entrenching tool on the web belt along with a poncho liner at the back.

The BGM-71 TOW (Tube-launched, Optically tracked, Wire-guided) is the anti-tank missile that replaced the M40 shown above. In this photograph, it is obviously a hot day at Fort Jackson, as soldiers have rolled-up sleeves and shirts untucked. This is consistent with a high wet bulb temperature, a gauge of heat and humidity conditions monitored closely to prevent heat-related injuries during training.

During the 1950s, the brown-shoe Army transitioned into a force that required black boots for the uniform. Savvy soldiers kept a pair of boots perpetually shined for inspections and a pair that were destined for everyday wear or the field. The last thing a soldier wanted to hear during an inspection was, "Did you shine these with a Hershey bar?"

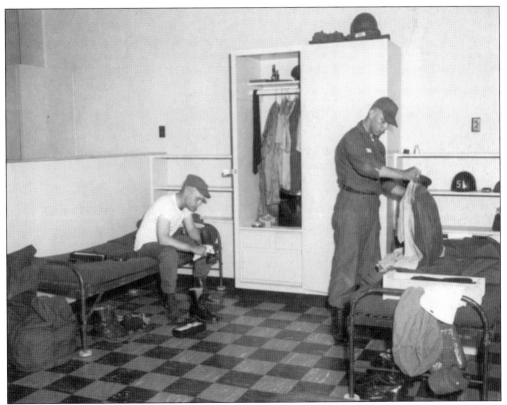

This 1966 barracks photograph shows the aforementioned soldier's least favorite activity in action—polishing those black boots. If one hangs around soldiers long enough, one will hear of many different methods and ingredients for optimum boot polishing—water, alcohol, fire, even floor wax—anything but the expected answer of basic black polish from a Kiwi can and a buffing cloth.

The pictured mock-ups were manufactured in 1967 by the 3rd US Army Training Aids Center to facilitate training in the use of the UH-1D Huey and CH-47 Chinook helicopters. With the ever-increasing use of helicopters in the Vietnam War and the expectation that the majority of the infantry troops in training were destined for that theater, training in the safe and expeditious disembarking of such aircraft was a necessary skill. Although rotary-wing aircraft had been in use in the military since the Korean War in the early 1950s, their role then had been primarily for medical evacuations and supply. The Vietnam War saw the Army incorporate air operations via helicopters into its fighting doctrine, placing troops into the thick of action and later extracting them when their mission was complete.

A Vietnamese log house is explained to a group of Vietnam replacements by M.Sgt. Joe Lowe. Master Sergeant Lowe, an instructor with the 3rd Training Brigade, explains that the log house is the main shelter for Montagnard tribesmen. The log house was one of several authentic houses provided in the simulated Vietnamese village used in the ninth week of AIT. This simulated village, named Bau Bang, was built from March to September 1966 by 3rd Brigade personnel in their off-duty time. The village was a composite of living conditions and types of construction commonly found in Vietnamese villages and hamlets and was designed to give the AIT students a forecast of what they might expect when they went to Vietnam. The ominous moat with punji stakes shown below was designed to guard the hamlet from a frontal assault.

Capt. Martin Pierce provides information and interprets for South Vietnamese Army officers as they view first aid training given to basic combat trainees. Mouth-to-mouth resuscitation was the topic this day. During the Vietnam War, South Vietnamese military personnel were frequent visitors and often classmates to American soldiers in courses that encompassed all military occupational specialties.

A dummy is hoisted up to the helicopter in a medical evacuation exercise. In late 1966, AIT was increased from eight to nine weeks to include more Republic of Vietnam–oriented training. Around this time, the M16 rifle replaced the M14 as the primary weapon of the infantry soldier.

Pictured here are enlisted men's family quarters around 1966. A 1999 RAND report indicated that "service members choose to live on-base primarily for economic reasons. The preference for on-base housing is driven by the perceived gap between the local market value of government housing and the allowances provided for those who occupy civilian quarters. While service members consider the traditional benefits of military housing (e.g., support, cohesiveness) useful to families in general, they do not regard them as decisive in choosing whether to live on- or off-base. Fewer military families than civilian families own homes; when renting, both spend about the same proportion of their salaries on housing." Since this era, family housing has been upgraded several times from what is pictured here.

Recruits train on the M203 grenade launcher, which attaches below the barrel of the M16 rifle. As an anti-personnel weapon, the M203 is quite effective in dispersing tear gas in riot conditions or shooting explosive rounds. Other applications of the M203 include rounds that light up the battlefield for short periods of time and rounds for marking locations of soldiers on the ground.

The ever-increasing impact of tanks and other armored vehicles in World War II necessitated the design of more portable weapons to defend against them. The M203 grenade launcher was not designed for armored vehicles, but a similar small weapons system that could be easily deployed with foot soldiers was deemed optimal. The result in 1963 was the M72 Light Anti-Tank Weapon, or LAW.

The advent of the all-volunteer force in 1973 made a large difference in the numbers of women coming into the regular and reserve components of the Army. As a result of recruitment, training, and greater opportunities, the total number of WACs in the Army increased from 12,260 in 1972 to 52,900 in 1978.

Women trainees are drilled in the proper method of challenging while on guard duty. The women's barracks are pictured in the background. The Women's Army Corps was disbanded in 1978, and all units were then integrated with male units. WACs at that time converted to the branch for whichever military occupational specialty they worked in.

In 1975, the Army chief of staff approved the consolidation of basic training for men and women when test programs showed that "female graduates met the standards in every area except the Physical Readiness Training Program," which could be modified without compromising the value of training. By 1977, combined basic training became policy, and men and women began integrating in the same basic training units in September.

The 1970s saw many changes in the integration of women into the armed forces. Women were allowed to enter the Army Reserve Officers Training Program (ROTC) beginning in September 1972. Involuntary discharge of military women because of pregnancy and parenthood was eliminated in June 1975. In 1976, the first women were admitted to the US Military Academy at West Point. By 1979, all enlistment qualifications were the same for men and women

The M18A1 Claymore is an anti-personnel mine that has been in use since 1960. It has generated a reputation as being "Army proof," in that the Army has made it so simplistic it is difficult to mess up. Notice the warning on the mine in the lower photograph, which states vividly "Front toward enemy." But despite the seeming ridiculousness of this, the mine is a deadly tool, showering the unfortunate recipient of its charge with a volley of steel balls, similar to a shotgun blast. Generations of basic trainees have learned the basics of the claymore. The photograph above is from 1982, while the one below is from 1994.

This trainee practices placement of the M21 anti-tank mine. This mine is capable of taking out a tank that rumbles over it. It is often detonated by the tank kicking back an attached tilt rod, which activates the fuse mechanism, setting off the mine and driving its steel plate through the armor.

This 1980 photograph shows a two-man crew manning the M2 .50-caliber machine gun, which has been used extensively since 1933 as a light infantry weapon as well as being mounted to vehicles and for aircraft armament. The list of wars and conflicts around the globe that this weapon has been utilized in can fill a history book.

The simplest item of equipment carried by soldiers can also be the most versatile and indispensable: the entrenching tool, or "e-tool." Pictured here is the modern version, an all-steel tri-folding e-tool with D-shaped handle. The latest lightweight plastic tri-fold design is 20 percent lighter than the all-steel tri-fold: 1.5 pounds instead of 2.25 pounds.

This female soldier in 1991 showcases the state-of-the-art uniform for its time, with Kevlar helmet, battle dress uniform (BDU), and poncho in woodland camouflage pattern. This uniform debuted in 1981, replacing the old olive drab fatigues that had dressed the Army since 1952. In 2004, soldiers began wearing the newly minted Army combat uniform (ACU), the successor to the BDU. It is the current utility uniform.

Fort Jackson's 282nd Army Band, which dates to service in Richmond, Virginia, in 1869 as the 21st Infantry Band, was originally deactivated in 1949 at Seoul, South Korea. In March 1956, the band was reactivated at Fort Jackson. Similar to the regimental band in the World War I era, the band plays graduations and other ceremonies, including funerals, promotions, and retirement parades, on behalf of the military. By doctrine, the band has a secondary mission to augment military police operations during combat, providing perimeter security in areas where enemy prisoners of war are collected and held for further processing. Notice the ornate accoutrements of the drum major wielding his ceremonial mace while leading the band down the parade field. The mace is used in relaying commands to the band members.

Since 1973, Victory Tower has been a mainstay of Fort Jackson's basic training. It is one of the first challenges that new recruits face when they begin the journey toward becoming soldiers. The 40-foot tower with rappelling and climbing challenges requires recruits to face their fears early on, and it gives the drill sergeant a sense of what each individual soldier is capable of.

Victory Tower has seen its share of letdowns. For every soldier who successfully completes the tower on the first try, there are many who freeze at the top and cannot go on. Somehow, though, they persevere and put forth the effort to prove to their drill sergeants that they are as committed to finishing basic as they were when they signed on.

Hilton Field is the culmination of basic training. The day before graduation is designated Family Day, when the battalion commander meets with family members and friends of graduating soldiers to discuss their recent experiences and answer questions. Family and friends can also meet the unit's drill sergeants and observe demonstrations of soldier skills. Graduation is the following day at 9:00 or 10:00 a.m., depending upon the season. Hilton Field was renovated in 2013, and the Gen. Andrew Jackson statue was moved there from Gate One. The new main entrance features an elaborate archway to welcome friends and family members. Other improvements include resurfaced roads, a paved parking area, an upgraded sound system, and improved restroom facilities. State and territorial flag displays, improved brickwork, and new signage all contribute toward giving the first-time visitor a great impression of Fort Jackson.

Six

THE WAR ON TERROR

As the saying goes, the journey begins with a first step. In the world of the recruit, basic training begins with the reception battalion. All the administrative stuff gets out of the way immediately: processing medical, financial, and personnel paperwork; getting a physical exam, shots, haircut, uniform, and Army physical fitness uniform (APFU); and taking the first physical training (PT) test.

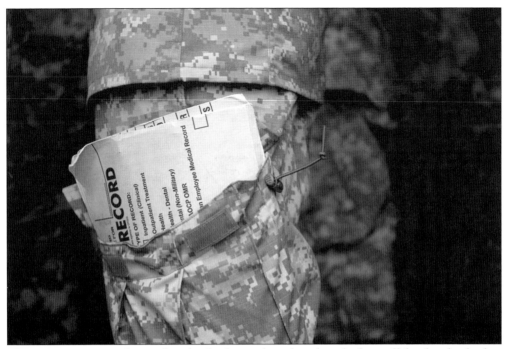

The average recruit might wonder what hit him or her when disembarking off that bus for the first time. Despite what they might be thinking, the administrative part comes first. Moving from station to station within the Reception Battalion, recruits lay the foundation for the rest of their careers, setting up records that will follow them through their entire time in the Army.

Hurry up and wait is the watchword, and recruits might as well enjoy this respite from what is to come. The Army does not want recruits to fail and hence does not overtax them with responsibilities or physical tasks they cannot handle at this time. The focus is on getting all these seemingly boring details out of the way first.

This reception phase typically lasts the first week and is where initial preparations for training are performed, including a haircut (head shave or buzz cut for men; women must either cut their hair short or wear it pinned up); a physical examination and shots; the distribution of uniforms and personal gear; and instruction in basic marching, as well as the upkeep of the barracks and personal locker and space. Of course, recruits who fail the physical assessment test can be held back at Reception Battalion, where they are placed in a fitness training company (FTC), sometimes referred to jokingly as "Fat Camp." Recruits in FTC are given two chances per week to complete the physical assessment test and upon passing are allowed to move on to begin their formal basic training.

Basic training is divided into Red, White, and Blue Phases. Reception is included in the first days of Red Phase, alternately known as Week Zero. During Red Phase, a recruit's every action is observed and corrected by drill sergeants, if necessary. This phase helps the recruit to develop an acute attention to detail as well as a sense of common responsibility to the unit. Land navigation is just one of the subjects of Red Phase.

Availability of GPS for finding one's way is not always a guarantee. Therefore, one of the earliest drills of Red Phase finds the recruit engaging in map reading, land navigation, and compass use. These skills are tested at the Compass Course, where recruits are divided into groups and must navigate their way to a series of points throughout a wooded area.

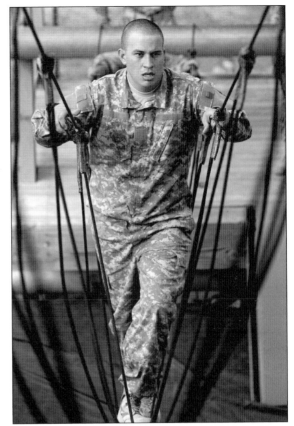

Continuing in the first week of Red Phase, recruits attempt other physical challenges including the imposing Victory Tower. Recruits must navigate through several obstacles at extreme heights, including climbing and negotiating rope ladders and bridges. They must then rappel down a 40-foot wall (back-first, attached to a rope harness). Challenging one's fear of heights is not an insignificant feat. The confidence in overcoming this fear is instrumental to the recruits' advancement and sets the stage for team-oriented challenges to come. More than one drill sergeant has said that recruits cannot contribute productively to a team until they have confidence in their own abilities.

In the Teamwork Development Course, or TDC, recruits are members of squads that must negotiate a series of obstacles, with emphasis on working as a team rather than as individuals. In this scenario, team members must successfully scale a wall before moving on to overcome other obstacles along their path. Teammates assess the problem for about five minutes before being allowed 20 minutes to carry out their plan.

Continuing this scenario, after making it over the wall, teammates negotiate an obstacle by using boards to create a bridge. Experience has shown that some groups succeed at the task, but most do not. The intent of the TDC is not necessarily "winning" the event but rather development of a teamwork mentality. The recruits, through problem-solving activities, learn to trust each other in a collaborative environment.

First-aid training is also given during this period. Recruits are trained in evaluating and properly treating casualties, ranging from the simple dressing of a wound to application of a tourniquet. Recruits are also trained in how to evaluate and treat heat casualties such as dehydration. In this photograph, soldiers prepare a casualty for evacuation.

Secured to a stretcher, the casualty can be safely moved to another location, preferably to a medical treatment facility that can fully assess and treat his wounds. Successful first aid administered as soon as is practicable is said to help reduce eventual casualties by as much as 15 percent on the battlefield.

In 2010, the Army overhauled basic combat training to reflect changes in the modern battlefield. Bayonet training was abandoned, and traditional combatives were reconfigured to focus on hand-to-hand fighting and handheld weapons. Pugil stick training, as shown here, simulates fighting with a rifle in that one of the ends signifies where a bayonet would be. The other end is the butt stock.

The training session allows recruits to practice fighting with a rifle in a safe, controlled environment, complete with groin protectors, padded gloves, and football helmets. Recruits learn to function when faced with stress and violence, and the training prepares them to deliver a blow and take a blow. As with most of the recruits' new experiences, it is also an opportunity to gain confidence in their newfound abilities.

Nuclear, biological, and chemical (NBC) training remains constant with every new generation of soldier. As in World War II, troops train for gas attacks, if only because the memory of World War I's experience shows that the enemy might resort to such violence. The technology might change, but the basic training experience remains the same.

Soldiers exit the gas chamber. Without the masks' protection, they experience upper respiratory distress, tearing eyes, and skin irritation. The gas used in the chamber is chlorobenzylidene malononitrile, known as CS. Symptoms subside within 30 minutes after leaving the chamber, but care must be used since any particles of gas that have lodged in fabrics can be active up to a week later. A thorough washing of uniforms is definitely prescribed.

The confidence course occurs in the White Phase of basic training and consists of 24 stations requiring individual effort or team collaboration with inspiring names like the Tough Nut, the Skyscraper, the Belly Robber, and the Wall Hanger. As with other challenges the recruits face, they must use their problem-solving abilities and physical endurance to master the course.

A 7.62-millimeter round is ejected as a recruit fires his weapon for record in the White Phase. In the past, new soldiers would learn to shoot their weapons and qualify with the Army's red-dot close-combat optic sight. But due to fears of electronic warfare increasing in the future battlefield, leaders now stress the importance of making sure soldiers can operate in technology-degraded environments.

The Army Physical Fitness Test (APFT) uses three events to measure physical fitness. Passing the APFT is a requirement for graduating basic combat training. Standards are increasing for future years, however. The new six-event test will keep the two-mile run from the current APFT but scraps the push-ups and sit-ups in favor of leg tucks, a medicine ball power throw, three-rep max dead lift, "T" push-ups, and a shuttle sprint-drag-carry.

The culminating events of basic training in the Blue Phase include the "field problems" and field training exercises (FTX), such as nighttime combat operations, and military operations in urban terrain (MOUT) training, which combines all previously taught basic combat skills to complete teamwork exercises and missions. The drill sergeants make the experience as realistic as possible, throwing obstacles in the recruits' paths and trying to thwart plans.

This is it, the final day recruits have waited for—graduation from basic training! Family and friends have assembled at Hilton Field to watch them march into view and claim their titles as soldiers. Those 10 weeks of basic have seen recruits become people they might not have ever thought they could become. They found new sources of stamina and resilience in themselves while honing their decision-making skills in ways unheard of before they entered Fort Jackson. They made new friends and found within themselves a core of confidence and strength they can rely upon as they embark on the next phase of their new career. Yes, they will take it all in, for they have earned it. Congratulations, soldiers!

Seven

HEROES AND HISTORY

The 100th Infantry Division's combat record was associated with World War II. Activated too late in World War I to deploy, the division was deactivated in 1919 but in the 1920s was assigned to the reserve component. Prior to World War II, the 100th was deactivated again, but it was reactivated in November 1942 and saw extensive service in Europe. (Author's collection.)

Originally the 1st New Jersey Cavalry Regiment and renamed the 102nd Cavalry in August 1921, the regiment was inducted into federal service in January 1941. It saw combat in northwest Europe during World War II, fighting in the Normandy, northern France, Rhineland, Ardennes-Alsace, and central Europe campaigns. Following the war, the 102nd was inactivated in October 1945. The regiment was released from active federal service in July 2009 following a series of postwar reorganizations. (Author's collection.)

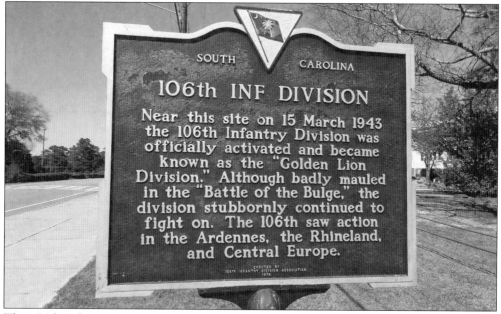

The 106th Infantry Division was activated in March 1943 for service in Europe. It became known as the "Golden Lion" Division due to its distinctive shoulder patch. The 106th suffered the indignity of surrender during the Battle of the Bulge, but the unit's stories of heroism in the face of confinement as POWs are inspiring. (Author's collection.)

Based in Charlotte, North Carolina, the 108th has led several different lives before settling in as an Army Reserve training division. In January 1991, more than 300 soldiers from the 108th were called to active duty to support Operation Desert Storm, marking the first mobilization ever for members of the division. The soldiers assisted in the retraining of individual soldiers at Fort Jackson who were recalled to military duty. (Author's collection.)

108th DIVISION

The "Golden Griffon" Division was created in 1946 as the 108th Airborne Division of the Army Reserve. It was reorganized as an infantry division in 1952, as a training division in 1956, and as an institutional training division in 1993. It has trained Fort Jackson soldiers since the early 1950s and mobilized units here for active service in 1991 and 2001.

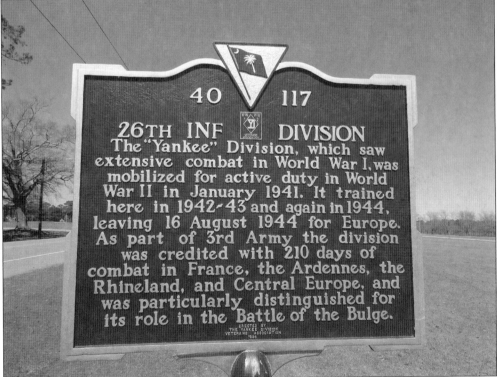

40 117

26TH INF DIVISION

The "Yankee" Division, which saw extensive combat in World War I, was mobilized for active duty in World War II in January 1941. It trained here in 1942-43 and again in 1944, leaving 16 August 1944 for Europe. As part of 3rd Army the division was credited with 210 days of combat in France, the Ardennes, the Rhineland, and Central Europe, and was particularly distinguished for its role in the Battle of the Bulge.

Activated from the National Guard, the 26th Infantry Division, nicknamed the "Yankee Division" due to its ties to the northeastern United States, served in Europe in both world wars. During World War II, the division helped liberate the Mauthausen-Gusen concentration camp complex in southern Germany and Austria. After the war, the division returned to the National Guard from 1947 until 1993. (Author's collection.)

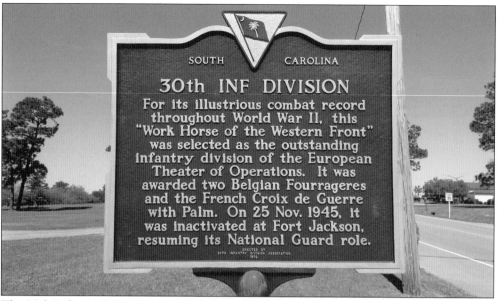

The 30th Infantry Division was called the "Old Hickory" Division in honor of Pres. Andrew Jackson. Regarded by a noted Army historian as the number-one infantry division in the European theater, the 30th was involved in 282 days of intense combat from June 1944 through April 1945. Reverting to National Guard status after the war, the division was inactivated on January 4, 1974. (Author's collection.)

The 31st Infantry Division was known as the "Dixie" Division, composed of soldiers from the deep South. Training at Fort Jackson for much of World War II, the division was not deployed until 1944, when it was sent to the Pacific. The division was mobilized during the Korean War but never went overseas. In 1968, the division was inactivated, with its units becoming part of the 30th Armored Division. (Author's collection.)

Based today in Fort Carson, Colorado, the 4th Division was mobilized in both world wars, seeing action in France, Belgium, and Germany. During the early days of the Cold War, the 4th Division was a member of the first NATO contingent in Europe. The 4th also saw action in the Vietnam and Iraq Wars. (Author's collection.)

SOUTH CAROLINA

4TH INFANTRY DIVISION

Organized in 1917, the 4th Infantry Division was stationed in this area at Ft. Jackson during World War II and received its final training here for the June 6, 1944 D-Day invasion of Normandy. The division was one of the first on the beaches. The 4th was also in other campaigns, including the Siegfried Line, Hurtgen Forest, and Battle of the Bulge.

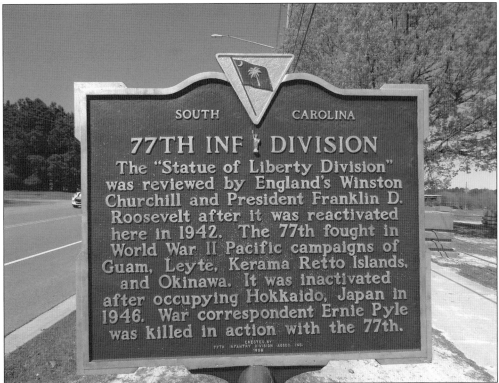

SOUTH CAROLINA

77TH INF DIVISION

The "Statue of Liberty Division" was reviewed by England's Winston Churchill and President Franklin D. Roosevelt after it was reactivated here in 1942. The 77th fought in World War II Pacific campaigns of Guam, Leyte, Kerama Retto Islands, and Okinawa. It was inactivated after occupying Hokkaido, Japan in 1946. War correspondent Ernie Pyle was killed in action with the 77th.

The 77th was the first American division composed of draftees to arrive in France in World War I, landing in April 1918. Ordered back into service in 1942, the division distinguished itself in the Western Pacific. The lineage of the 77th Infantry Division continues today with the 77th Sustainment Brigade (US Army Reserve), with its headquarters at Fort Dix, New Jersey. In 2011, the brigade deployed to Iraq in support of Operation New Dawn. (Author's collection.)

The 81st, credited with being the originator of the first distinctive shoulder patch for Army units, saw action in France in World War I and in the Pacific in World War II. Today, the patch is worn by soldiers of the 81st Regional Support Command at Fort Jackson. (Author's collection.)

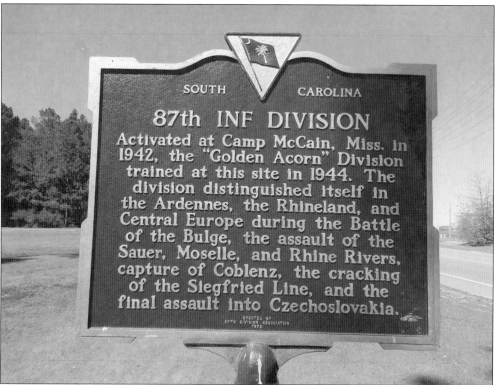

The 87th Division's distinctive shoulder patch was a gold-colored acorn. The division saw no combat after arriving overseas in September 1918 but was utilized in a general support role. In World War II, the division saw significant action at the Battle of the Bulge and was preparing to deploy to Japan when the war ended. After the war, the 87th served as an Army Reserve support command until 2015. (Author's collection.)

The 8th Infantry Division served in both world wars and in Operation Desert Storm. During World War II, the division landed in Normandy after the D-Day invasion and took part in several campaigns, including the Battle of Hurtgen Forest. The division helped liberate a concentration camp in northern Germany and later spent decades during the Cold War in Germany until inactivation in 1992. (Author's collection.)

Cpl. Freddie Stowers was born and raised in Sandy Springs, South Carolina, and was part of the first military draft of World War I. In 1991, he was posthumously awarded the Medal of Honor for his valor during World War I. The single soldier billeting complex on Fort Jackson is named after him, and a statue of him was dedicated in November 2015 outside Anderson University's Thrift Library in South Carolina. (Courtesy of Wikipedia Creative Commons License.)

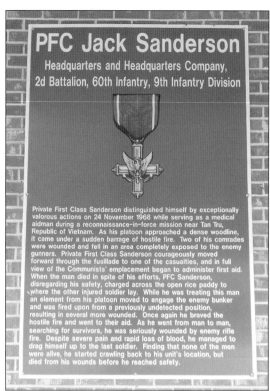

PFC Jack Sanderson is proof that heroes come in all shapes, sizes, races, and military occupational specialties. A native of New York, Sanderson distinguished himself in battle as a combat medic during a skirmish in Vietnam as a member of the 9th Infantry Division. His actions merited the posthumous award of the Distinguished Service Cross. Sanderson Hall at Fort Jackson is proudly named in his honor. (Author's collection.)

This athletic field on Fort Jackson is named after the creator of the Army Rangers and the first commander of the original Ranger battalion. Brig. Gen. William O. Darby briefly served at Fort Jackson with the 80th Division. He modelled the Rangers after British Commandos. He served with distinction in North Africa and in Italy. Darby, aged 34 at the time of his death, was posthumously promoted to brigadier general on May 15, 1945. (Author's collection.)

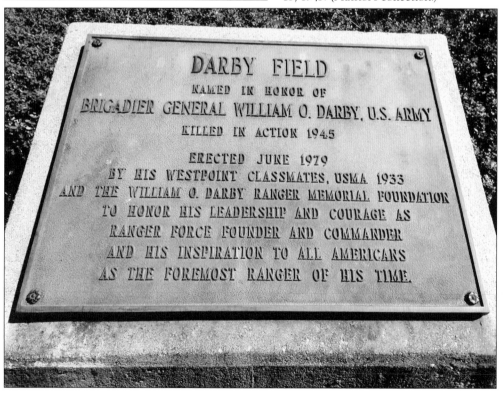

World War I was such a time of patriotic fervor that countless pieces of music were written to entice the listener to join up or buy some war bonds. The Library of Congress, where this piece of music was found, contains over 13,500 annotated pieces of World War I music. This song, though not as famous as "Over There," no doubt inspired its hometown audience. (Courtesy of Library of Congress.)

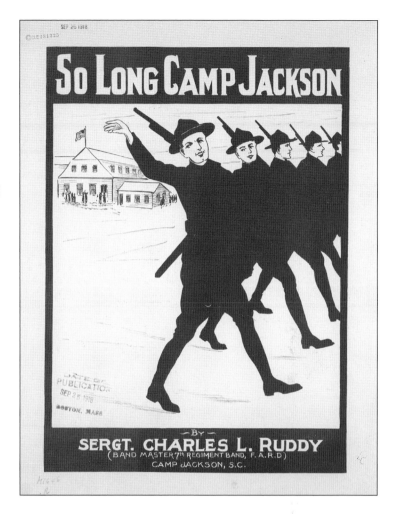

A pennant is normally a commemorative flag typically used to show support for a particular athletic team. But this pennant showcases Fort Jackson, South Carolina. Traditionally, pennants were made of felt and fashioned in the official colors of a particular team. By this definition, the background should have been olive drab green to celebrate the Army's presence on the fort. Instead it is a rather dramatic white with red lettering. (Author's collection.)

This souvenir dates to the 1960s, featuring the sounds of basic training. Such novelties were considered high tech for the era and gave the listener a taste of the basic training cycle. These records were manufactured for all military branches; the author's brother sent one home that featured the sounds of his Air Force basic training. (Author's collection.)

Designed like a typical high school yearbook, this publication sums up a soldier's basic training experience in a concise format, complete with action photographs and individual "class" photographs for each platoon involved in the training cycle. From decade to decade, it seems the only changes were the uniforms and weapons used by the trainees, not to mention the addition of color to the package sometime in the 1970s. (Author's collection.)

World War II was the heyday for this souvenir. There seems to have been a plentiful supply of these pillowcases in many varieties just begging to have a military post or ship's name emblazoned upon their faces. With so many draftees, is it any wonder that soldiers and sailors would pour out their hearts to their mom, best girl, or even a sister with the sentiments contained herein? (Author's collection.)

In 1953, this field was named after Sgt. Richmond Hobson Hilton. Sergeant Hilton, a native of Westville in Kershaw County, South Carolina, earned the Medal of Honor as a result of his actions on October 11, 1918, while serving with M Company, 118th Infantry "Palmetto" Regiment, a South Carolina National Guard unit fighting with the Army Expeditionary Forces in Europe. Hilton Field is seen here in 1985.

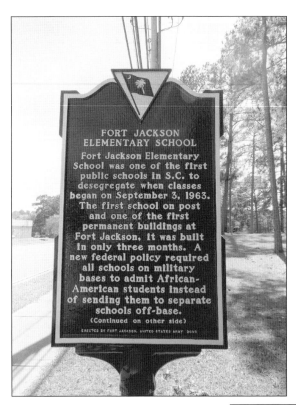

Fort Jackson Elementary School was the first desegregated school in South Carolina, opening in September 1963 in the midst of the Civil Rights era. Up until that time, the family members of Fort Jackson soldiers had to attend the segregated schools off-post in the Columbia area. The opening of the school preceded Pres. Lyndon Johnson's Civil Rights Act of 1964, which outlawed segregation nationwide in public facilities. Later renamed Hood Street Elementary, the school remained in use until 2007, when it was closed by the Department of Defense School System due to declining enrollment. Today, the building houses the US Army Signal Network Enterprise Center. (Both, author's collection.)

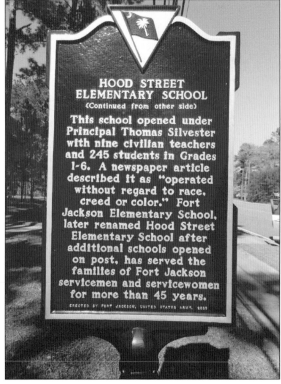

Eight

FORT JACKSON NATIONAL CEMETERY

In July 2007, construction began on the Fort Jackson National Cemetery in Columbia. The cemetery was dedicated on October 26, 2008. It encompasses 585 acres obtained from Fort Jackson. Although the name reflects Fort Jackson, the post does not own or control the cemetery. The Department of Veterans Affairs is responsible for the management and upkeep of the facility. (Author's collection.)

The grounds of Fort Jackson National Cemetery were opened for burials in January 2009, and final construction was completed in June 2015. The 50-acre interment area provides 5,704 full-casket gravesites including 4,224 pre-placed crypts, 1,085 in-ground cremation sites, and 2,000 columbarium niches. Fort Jackson National Cemetery is the third national cemetery established in South Carolina and the 126th in the national cemetery system. Burial in a national cemetery is open to all members of the armed forces who have met a minimum active duty service requirement and were discharged under conditions other than dishonorable. A veteran's spouse, widow or widower, minor dependent children, and, under certain conditions, unmarried adult children with disabilities may also be eligible for burial. Eligible spouses and children may be buried even if they predecease the veteran. Members of the reserve components of the armed forces who die while on active duty, who die while on training duty, or who were eligible for retired pay, may also be eligible for burial. (Author's collection.)

Since January 1, 2000, Section 578 of Public Law 106-65 of the National Defense Authorization Act has mandated that the US armed forces shall provide a military funeral for any eligible veteran if requested by his or her family. It states: "An honor guard detail for the burial of an eligible veteran shall consist of no fewer than two members of the Armed Forces. One member of the detail shall be a representative of the parent armed service of the deceased veteran. The honor guard detail will, at a minimum, perform a ceremony that includes the folding and presenting of the flag of the United States to the next of kin and the playing of 'Taps' which will be played by a lone bugler, if available, or by audio recording." (Both, courtesy of South Carolina National Guard.)

The military takes great care to ensure proper decorum for military funeral honors, including trained personnel; implementation of standardized procedures; dignified, respectful honor guard details; professional dress and appearance; synchronization of movement; and regular quality control of funeral details. Providing military funeral honors is designated as a "total force mission," meaning that other armed service members may preside over military funerals, though the military strives to include at least one representative of the deceased soldier's branch of service to participate in the services. Most often, in such cases, it is this single representative of the deceased's service who will present the flag. (Courtesy of South Carolina National Guard.)

The three-volley salute honors the deceased at military funerals. The honor guard fires its weapons in a consecutive set of three volleys. The firearm used is typically an M1 or M14 rifle. At ceremonial occasions, these rifles look more traditional in appearance and are generally favored over contemporary firearms like the M16, in keeping with the dignity of the ceremony. The Department of Veterans Affairs, in its fact sheet on gun salutes, states: "The custom originates from the European dynastic wars, where the fighting ceased so the dead and wounded could be removed. Then, three shots were fired into the air to signal that the battle could resume." (Both, courtesy of South Carolina National Guard.)

The Department of Veterans Affairs, in its fact sheet on "Taps," states that Capt. John Francis Tidball, a Civil War artillery commander, began the custom of playing the song at military funerals. In early July 1862 at Harrison's Landing, a corporal of Tidball's Battery A, 2nd US Artillery, died. Tidball wanted the soldier buried with full military honors but was refused permission to fire seven rifles three times (a 21-shot salute) over the grave so as to not reveal their position to the enemy. Instead, he had "Taps" played at the man's services. While "Taps" had originated as a French bugle call to have troops return to the unit after a night of drinking, it evolved into the lights-out call that ends the Army's day. By 1891, the Army had rewritten its funeral procedures so that "Taps" would be standard. (Both, courtesy of South Carolina National Guard.)

The National Cemetery Administration ensures that "A United States flag is provided, at no cost, to drape the casket or accompany the urn of a deceased veteran who served honorably in the armed forces. The flag that drapes the casket of the deceased veteran honors the memory of his or her service to the country." The flag is placed on the closed casket so the blue field is at the head and over the left shoulder of the deceased. The ceremonial folding and presentation of this flag is a moving tribute of lasting importance to the veteran's family. Generally, after "Taps" is played, the flag is folded into the familiar triangular shape and then presented to the appropriate family member. (Both, courtesy of South Carolina National Guard.)

According to the American Legion's website "American Flag-Folding Procedures," "The flag of the United States draped over the casket is precisely folded thirteen times by a total of six honor guards, three on each side of the casket. When the flag is completely folded, the stars point upwards, which remind Americans of their national motto, In God We Trust. After the flag is completely folded and tucked in, it takes on the appearance of a tri-cornered hat, reminding Americans of the soldiers who served under General George Washington, and the sailors and Marines who served under Captain John Paul Jones, who were followed by their comrades and shipmates in the United States Armed Forces." (Both, courtesy of South Carolina National Guard.)

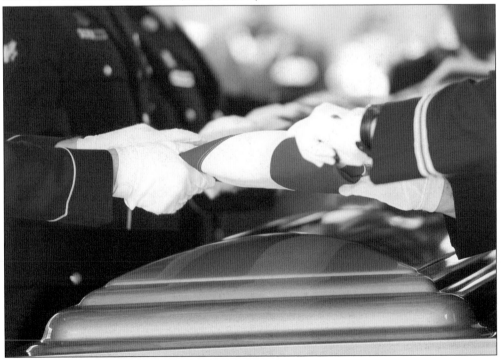

The article continues, "Upon completion of folding the flag, the officer in charge of the honor guard hands the flag to the presenting officer to give to the deceased's family. The flag will show no red or white stripes, leaving only the blue field with stars. The presenting officer will hold the flag waist-high with parallel hands, the flag residing against his up- and down-turned palms. The presenter leans forward while presenting the flag, the straight edge of the flag facing the recipient. The presenter then recites the following wording: 'On behalf of the President of the United States, the United States Army, and a grateful nation, please accept this flag as a symbol of our appreciation for your loved one's honorable and faithful service.' " (Both, courtesy of South Carolina National Guard.)

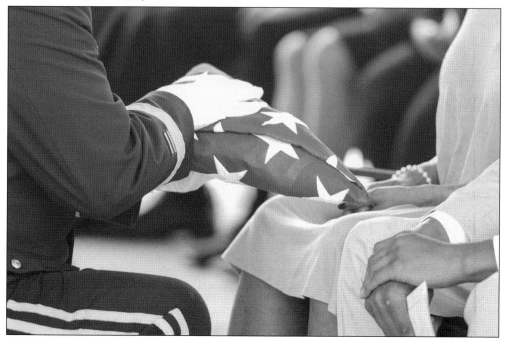

BIBLIOGRAPHY

"American Flag Folding Procedures." American Legion. Accessed July 5, 2019. www.legion.org/flag/folding.

Boyd, John A. "America's Army of Democracy: The National Army, 1917–1919." *Army History Magazine* 109 (Fall 2018): 6–27.

Buddin, Richard, Carol Roan Gresenz, Sue Hosek, et al. "An Evaluation of Housing Options for Military Families." RAND Report, 1999.

"Burial Flags." National Cemetery Administration. Accessed July 5, 2019. www.cem.va.gov/burial_benefits/burial_flags.asp.

Criswell, Stephen. "Benedict College." *South Carolina Encyclopedia.* University of South Carolina, Institute for Southern Studies. Accessed July 3, 2019. www.scencyclopedia.org/sce/entries/benedict-college/.

Edgar, Walter B., and Deborah K. Woodley. *Columbia: Portrait of a City.* Norfolk, VA: The Donning Company, 1986.

Hamilton, Brian. "Victory Tower Lays the Foundation for Basic Combat Training." Army.mil. June 13, 2016. www.army.mil/article/169530/victory_tower_lays_the_foundation_for_basic_combat_training.

Helsley, Alexia Jones. *Columbia, South Carolina: A History.* Charleston, SC: The History Press, 2015.

Hubbel, Julia E. "A Female Recruit's Day in the Life in Army Boot Camp." Medium.com. April 1, 2018.

Moore, John Hammond. "Nazi Troopers in South Carolina, 1944–1946." *South Carolina Historical Magazine* 81, no. 4 (October 1980): 306–315.

Roberts, Bryan. "Hilton Field Renovation Completed." Army.mil. April 18, 2013. www.army.mil/article/101366/hilton_field_renovation_completed.

Ruddy, Charles L. "So Long Camp Jackson." Score, 1918. Library of Congress. www.loc.gov/item/2007499439/.

Showalter, William Joseph. "The Geographical and Historical Environment of America's 32 New Soldier Cities." *National Geographic Magazine* 32, nos. 5 and 6, (November–December 1917): 438–476.

"The Story of Taps." US Department of Veterans Affairs. Accessed July 5, 2019. www.va.gov/opa/publications/celebrate/taps.pdf.

US Army Training Center, Infantry, Columbia, South Carolina. *50th Anniversary History 1917–1967, Fort Jackson, S.C.* Privately printed, 1967.

INDEX

DISCOVER THOUSANDS OF LOCAL HISTORY BOOKS FEATURING MILLIONS OF VINTAGE IMAGES

Arcadia Publishing, the leading local history publisher in the United States, is committed to making history accessible and meaningful through publishing books that celebrate and preserve the heritage of America's people and places.

Find more books like this at
www.arcadiapublishing.com

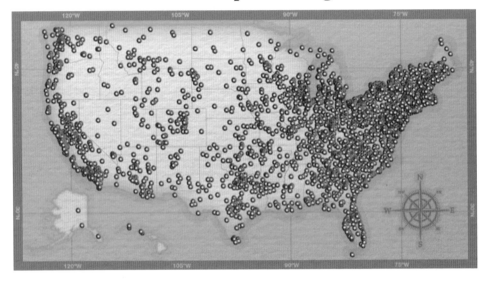

Search for your hometown history, your old stomping grounds, and even your favorite sports team.